Country park visitor surveys

Lessons from a study at Sherwood Forest and
Rufford Country Parks, Nottinghamshire
by
Stephen Locke

Published by:
Countryside Commission
John Dower House
Crescent Place
Cheltenham, Glos. GL50 3RA
Tel: (0242) 521381
© Countryside Commission 1985

Distributed by:
Countryside Commission
Publications Despatch Department
19/23 Albert Road
Manchester M19 2EQ
CCP 180
Price £3.25 including postage

Foreword

One of the keys to effective management of any recreation site is accurate information about who uses the site, and what attracted them to it. This report explains how Nottinghamshire County Council set about obtaining this information with the assistance of the Countryside Commission. The results for Sherwood Forest and Rufford Country Parks will be of interest to other country park managers as will be the description of the strengths and weaknesses of the methods used.

The research on which this report is based was carried out for Nottinghamshire County Council and the Countryside Commission by Social and Community Planning Research. Stephen Locke, the author of the report, is a Senior Project Officer with **Holiday Which?**

The Countryside Commission and Nottinghamshire County Council have been pleased to collaborate on a project which has enabled us to understand more about leisure in the countryside.

Contents

British Library Cataloguing in Publication Data

Locke, Stephen
   Country park visitor surveys: lessons from a
   study at Sherwood Forest and Rufford Country Parks.
   1. Parks — England — Nottinghamshire — Visitors
   I. Title
   306'.48'094252 SB484.G7   ISBN 0 86170 116 X

Set in 10/11pt Goudy Old Style by CGS Studios, Cheltenham and printed on Armageddon recycled paper by Severnprint, Gloucester.

IM/1/85

1. How the study came about

Who visits country parks? Why do they go? What do visitors do when they get there? How much money do they spend? And what do they think of the facilities on offer?

Natural curiosity about questions like these is understandable enough. But when, in May 1981, Nottinghamshire County Council embarked on a detailed survey of two of its three country parks, Sherwood and Rufford, it had deeper motives in mind. The Council's prime concern was to develop a base of hard information which it could use to improve the way it managed and promoted its country parks.

The Council's general approach

This quest for hard information had two main origins, one specific, one general. The first was the sequence of developments at Rufford Country Park. This park was bought by the Council in the early 1950s, but remained neglected and little used for many years. A major improvement programme — including the re-establishment of a large lake and the restoration of some buildings on the site — was set in hand during the 1970s, but it remained unclear whether emphasis of the programme was right.

The second motive behind the Sherwood/Rufford study was Nottinghamshire's growing belief that the public sector could improve its operations by adopting and developing techniques more usually associated with sound business practice. Some considerations — such as the profit motive — obviously didn't apply to many Council services. But the Council saw a great deal of potential in applying business methods of managing scarce resources. In particular, it was convinced that much could be learned from business expertise in maximising cost effectiveness within the constraints imposed by operating budgets. This need to improve the management of resources was held to apply just as much to country parks as to other public services. By the late 1970s, Nottinghamshire was spending roughly £600,000 on its country parks — or roughly 80p per visitor. But there was no basis for saying whether this money was being spent as effectively as it could be.

Rufford Country Park was seen as a particularly good candidate for Nottinghamshire's new approach. As a first step, the Council, with the support of the Countryside Commission, set in hand a study by management consultants Coopers and Lybrand, to look at questions such as

- the programme of development on the site. Were the right facilities being provided? Which potential white elephants should be avoided?
- the phasing of development on the site. Which facilities should come first, and which could wait?
- the way the site was promoted to the general public.

Coopers and Lybrand's report was published in March 1980. It made a range of specific proposals on the nature and phasing of development on the site; but its most important general conclusions were in the area of promotion. The report stressed in particular the need to develop a coherent promotional strategy for country parks, especially where there were no well established patterns of recreational use, or where facilities had recently been developed on a significant scale. One important practical outcome from all this was the appointment in 1980 of a marketing officer, to take responsibility for formulating a marketing strategy for Nottinghamshire's country parks — and for putting it into effect.

A strategy for promoting the parks

Following the Coopers and Lybrand study of Rufford Country Park — and taking into account a number of other factors — Nottinghamshire adopted a fourfold promotional strategy for 1981-82. This was applied not just to Rufford, but also to the Council's other two parks including nearby Sherwood Forest Country Park, where a new interpretive display had been developed in the existing visitor centre.

The four elements of this promotional strategy were

- to **increase general awareness** of visitor facilities in the park — so encouraging people to come (and spend money in the shop and catering facilities);
- to **increase mid-week use** of visitor facilities;
- to **extend the visitor season,** particularly into the spring and early autumn; and
- to **promote special events** and programmes, so helping to ensure their financial success and bring in repeat visitors to each park.

Each of these elements was expanded into a set of principles covering, for example, the need to

"overcome the 'bland' Sherwood Forest image by featuring specific facilities/attractions, and establishing reasons for visiting Sherwood Forest."

and the need to

"increase awareness of ability to spend money in Sherwood."

At the same time **target groups** were identified for each objective (such as retired people, holiday-makers and scheduled coach stops for the 'increased mid-week use' objective); specific **messages** were identified, including the identity and location of the area, its variety of attractions and activities for families; and appropriate **media** were selected — eg information posters, entries in guidebooks and signposting.

The Sherwood/Rufford study

To adopt a strategy is one thing, to put it into practice another. Nottinghamshire's promotional strategy, as outlined above, called for a level of management information the County simply did not possess. So, with the encouragement of (and financial support from) the Countryside Commission, Nottinghamshire decided to embark on a further, more detailed country park study. This one was to cover both Sherwood and Rufford, and was intended to provide detailed information under three main headings:

- **Monitoring of visitor use and expenditure,** in a way which could be related to other information on finances, manpower and physical resources of the parks, and which could be used by those responsible for managing the parks.
- **Information on visitors to the parks,** including where they came from, how they found out about the site, what

3

attracted them to it, what they did, the size of party, their age, sex and social group, and how often they came.

- **Evaluation of the promotional strategy,** by looking at the effect of different forms of promotion on visitors to the site, and by comparing their expectations with actual experiences; also by comparing awareness of the parks in the region as a whole — among visitors and non-visitors alike — before and after promotional campaigns.

All this was intended to contribute to Nottinghamshire's management strategy for the parks. But there was an important secondary objective, too. From the beginning, it was recognised that the survey would be breaking new ground, in the monitoring and evaluation of countryside recreation projects. So, as well as gathering data for Nottinghamshire's own use, those responsible for the survey knew they were testing a method from which others might learn.

Conclusion

The Sherwood/Rufford study was much more than a simple fact-gathering exercise. It was the product of a hard-headed approach which held that money spent on country parks — just like any other area of public service — needed to be subject to close scrutiny, to ensure that it was being spent as effectively as possible; and that business methods used in assessing cost-effectiveness had an important part to play.

The sequence of events leading up to the Sherwood/Rufford study — the 1970s programme of improvements to the Rufford site, the Coopers and Lybrand study of how the site might be developed and promoted, and the Council's subsequent adoption of a clearly-articulated promotional stategy for its country parks — may not of course be reproduced elsewhere. In any event, the sequence of events in Nottinghamshire — both before and after the Sherwood/Rufford survey — was in no sense a model for others to follow. Objectives have changed over time (for more about developments since the survey see p15); the list of parks covered by the Council's investigation and policy-making has varied; and the links between one stage and the next were fairly disjointed. One problem was that the Nottinghamshire marketing budget was reduced considerably after the survey was completed, making it harder to monitor the effectiveness of promotion on a continuing basis and restricting the amount of discretionary promotional spending indicated by the report's findings.

The background to the Sherwood/Rufford survey nonetheless illustrates two important general principles for those contemplating country park visitor surveys:

- **The need for clear management and promotional objectives for the parks concerned.** Without these, it is very difficult to set up an exercise which will provide useable results.
- **The need for firm ideas on how the survey results will be used.** General curiosity isn't really enough to justify the expense and effort involved: on the contrary, a properly designed exercise needs to start with a series of questions to which the survey can be made to provide clear, unambiguous answers.

2. How the survey was done

Nottinghamshire did not have the right resources of its own to carry out a survey of this kind, and it was decided at the outset to engage a firm of outside consultants. This chapter describes how the Council went about securing the services of a consultant, with the Countryside Commission's help, and the research methods the consultant used.

Tendering for the job

The wheels were set in motion with the circulation of a **project brief,** which was sent to four consultants known to have an interest in this kind of project. These organisations were invited to tender for the work by a specified date, and to set up an oral presentation for the steering committee of officials concerned.

The project brief was in five main parts:

- A description of the **background** to the proposed study, covering the Rufford marketing study, its conclusions, and the marketing approach the Council had subsequently adopted.
- A statement of the County's **promotional objectives** for its country parks (see p3).
- A synopsis of the **proposed research,** set out as a series of headings, with short notes on the methods envisaged — but stopping well short of detailed survey design.
- A note on **working arrangements,** describing who the consultants would be reporting to, and who they would be working with in the course of the project.
- A **timetable** for the background work, the field research, the write-up of the report, and its final presentation.

The contract for carrying out the survey was eventually given to Social and Community Planning Research (SCPR), an independent non-profit making institute registered as a charitable trust, and specialising in the design, conduct, analysis and interpretation of sample surveys. Much of SCPR's work is commissioned by government departments and local authorities.

Research methods

The research scheme proposed by SCPR, and eventually adopted for the survey, had two main elements:

- A **visitor self-completion survey,** designed to provide basic descriptive data on the visitors to each park at different times of year; and
- A **personal interview survey** of visitors to the visitor centres in each of the two parks.

(In addition, a programme of eight **group discussions** was set up, mainly to explore attitudes towards countryside recreation in general.

Two of these sessions were also used to help in the development of the personal interview survey questionnaire. But otherwise these discussions had little direct bearing on management strategy in two parks, ie the subject of the survey.)

Each part of the exercise was subjected to a **pilot survey** before the main work was done. This proved to be an important process, as it resulted in several modifications to the original plans.

The methods used are summarised in the table below.

Sherwood/Rufford visitor survey: Summary of research methods

	Self-completion questionnaire	Personal interview survey
Questionnaire used	Small single-sheet folded leaflets — see Appendix A. Handed out to visitors who were asked to return them to boxes provided.	14-page questionnaire — see Appendix B. Filled in by teams of trained interviewers in 15-minute sessions.
Typical questions	<ul><li>Where did you come from?</li><li>Have you read or heard about the country park in the last 6 months, in newspapers/on radio/on TV etc?</li><li>How many adults/males/females/people of different age groups in your party?</li><li>Any improvements you would like to see?</li></ul>	<ul><li>How did you like the parts of the park you visited?</li><li>How much money have you spent in the visitor centre?</li><li>How did you first come to hear about the park?</li><li>What prompted you to visit the park on this trip?</li><li>How has the park compared with what you expected?</li><li>What is your occupation?</li></ul>
Dates when work was done	Twelve representative days (see text) between September 1981 and August 1982.	Three weekends (Friday/Saturday/Sunday) between November 1981 and August 1982.
Visitors contacted	Drivers of all cars arriving at car parks (though a few vehicles were missed and there were a handful of refusals): 10,916 questionnaires issued altogether.	Random sample (see text) of adult visitors approached as they were about to leave visitor centres: 932 contacts made altogether.
Response rate	6,798 productive questionnaires received — 62 per cent of total issued.	624 interviews completed — 67 per cent of contacts made.
Problems encountered	<ul><li>Poor response rate to pilot survey — had to simplify leaflet, add more collecting bins and encourage visitors to complete at start of visit.</li><li>Some cars missed because of temporary traffic diversions.</li><li>Had to drop questions on job details because of poor response.</li><li>Questions about individual members of party had to be simplified.</li><li>Not possible to include coach parties.</li></ul>	<ul><li>For practical reasons, not possible to cover all visitors to parks — could only interview those passing through visitor centres.</li><li>15 minutes maximum per interviews</li><li>Hard to get useful response on expectation versus experiences.</li><li>Only limited comparisons between sub-groups possible, because of small sample size.</li></ul>
VERDICT	Despite initial practical problems, proved reasonably straightforward: good means of getting wealth of data at modest cost.	Data on occupational status and behaviour (particularly expenditure in visitor centres) very useful despite modest sample size; attempts to assess attitudes and expectations less successful.

5

The visitor self-completion survey

This was based on a short questionnaire — intentionally described to recipients as a 'leaflet' — which was handed out to each car driver as he or she drove into one of the car parks.

The questionnaire. The leaflet used is reproduced at Appendix A. The format was kept as simple as possible; it was simplified further following the pilot study and again after the first phase of the fieldwork proper. The leaflet consisted of a single A4 sheet printed on both sides, and folded into three. Most of the questions were designed to be answered by the car driver to whom the leaflet had been presented, and covered topics such as the recipient's starting point for the journey to the park, where the recipient had heard or read about the park and what he or she intended to do in the remainder of the visit. But one set of questions (numbers 5a to 5f) asked for information about all the members of the group, including whether they were male or female, how old they were, whether they had visited the park before, whether they were employed, unemployed, retired or engaged in full-time housework, and where they came from. This was done by setting out a grid containing boxes for the car driver and up to three other adults to answer each question.

The only open-ended question on the form was one which asked car drivers (but not the rest of the party) about any improvements they wanted to see. In the early stages of the fieldwork an attempt was made to ask about visitors' job details, so that socio-economic groupings could be coded; but this was not found to be workable, and this question had to be dropped in the later phases.

The questionnaire carried a Freepost address at the bottom for those who forgot to place it in one of the collecting bins; and bore a set of boxes for the interviewer to pre-code each copy before it was handed out.

Doing the fieldwork. The self-completion survey was carried out on 12 different days between September 1981 and August 1982. The days were carefully chosen to cover a mix of seasons, days of the week, school terms and holidays, bank holidays and days on which special events took place in the parks; fortunately, the 12 days chosen also represented a reasonable range of weather conditions.

On each of these 12 days, interviewers were stationed at each of the car parks on the two sites from 11am to 4pm. The interviewer approached each car as it entered, handed one questionnaire leaflet to the driver and urged respondents to complete it before walking off into the park. Several large clearly marked collecting bins were positioned around the car parks and around the visitor centres for the parks concerned. Each interviewer was accompanied by a counter whose job was to count the actual flow of traffic entering. Had this exceeded a certain level during any half hour period, the interviewer would have switched from universal distribution of questionnaires to sampling, by waiting three minutes after the previous contact before giving out another questionnaire; in the event this wasn't found necessary.

A total of 10,916 questionnaires were handed out in the 12 five-hour periods; and 6,800 useable completed ones were returned — a response rate of 62 per cent.

The personal interview survey

The broad intention behind the personal interview survey was

- to provide more detail on visitors arriving at the parks than could be obtained from the self-completion questionnaire;
- to find out about visitors' use of the parks; and
- to probe people's attitudes to, and expectations of, the parks.

Following the pilot survey, it was found necessary to reduce the length of each interview from 20-25 minutes to 15.

The questionnaire. This is reproduced at Appendix B. It was completed by teams of trained interviewers who read out from the list of 27 questions and recorded replies in spaces provided; many of the answers were coded on the spot.

The 27 questions covered a wide variety of topics. No-one was asked all 27: questions 9 to 13 were aimed only at first time visitors, and questions 14 to 19 only at repeat visitors.

The questions covered a wide variety of subjects. The **first sequence** asked visitors about their visit to the park: where they started from, how they got there, and how long they expected their visit to last. Respondents were then asked which part of the visitor centre they had been to (identified by means of pictures on a card), how they liked it, and how much money they had spent there. At the end of this sequence of questions, a filter question split out those who were on their first visit to the park from those who were making a repeat visit.

For first-time visitors to the park, the **second sequence** of questions focussed on the reasons for coming. How, and how long ago, did they first hear about the park? What prompted this visit? How did their experience of the park compare with what they expected? What plans did they have to return? For repeat visitors, the sequence was broadly similar, but there were additional questions on the number of previous visits and the date of the first visit.

The **third sequence** was again aimed at all visitors to the park, and dealt mainly with the impact of promotion and publicity on visitor behaviour. How often, in general, did the visitor make day trips? What publicity had the visitor seen? When, and by whom, was the decision made to visit the park? The questionnaire was concluded with a **fourth sequence** of questions on the characteristics of the visitor and the other members of his or her party — including age, sex, occupation, and access to a car.

As Appendix B shows, the questionnaire allowed for most of the information to be recorded in coded form. Prompts and other instructions to interviewers are given in capital letters under the question to which they relate.

Doing the fieldwork. The personal interview survey was carried out over three weekends (Friday/Saturday/Sunday) in November 1981, July 1982 and August 1982, between 11am and 4pm each day.

Practical arrangements had to be modified significantly following the pilot study. Originally it had been intended to interview a representative sample of all visitors to the parks, whether or not they had been to a visitor centre. But this wasn't found to be possible. As the survey was designed to assess (among other things) visitor reactions to facilities in the parks, there would have been no point interviewing visitors until at least half-way through their stay. In theory, it would have been best to interview visitors as they returned to their cars at the end of their stay. But

- visitors are likely to be pressed for time at this stage in their stay, and aren't going to be very willing to spare the time for an interview;
- it is difficult to take a representative sample of people who are arriving from all directions (as in a car park) rather than passing a specific point (eg an entrance or gateway). One option could have been to select a random sample of parked cars and wait for their occupants to return — but this would have required a lot of interviewers.

It was found that the only way to get round these problems was to ignore visitors to the parks who didn't enter the visitor centres, and concentrate instead on getting a representative sample of people who went into the centres.

The method used for obtaining this sample was very simple. No attempt was made to impose quotas on the sample, eg according to pre-determined proportions of people of a certain age or sex. Instead, the aim was solely to ensure that the selection of interviewees was automatic and left nothing to the discretion of the interviewer. On each day, interviewers were placed at a total of five contact points in and around the two parks' visitor centres. They started by approaching the first adult visitor to leave the centre past the contact point, and asking if he was at least half-way through his visit. If he was, the interview then proceeded, as set out in the questionnaire. As soon as the interview was over, the interviewer approached the very next person to pass the contact point. If people passed the contact point in a group, the policy was to approach the adult nearest to where the interviewer was standing.

This procedure then continued for the whole of the five-hour shift. Throughout this period, a count was taken of the number of adults passing the contact point, so that the response rate could be measured. This tally would also have made it possible to adjust the data collected in the personal interview survey to reflect all visitors to the centres during the survey period (though this facility wasn't eventually used).

During the 9 five-hour sessions, a total of 932 contacts were made using these sampling methods. Of these, 125 people refused to take part, and 183 were ineligible, eg because they had already been interviewed. This left a total of 624 interviews successfully completed, 67 per cent of the contacts made.

Conclusion

The two main parts of the exercise were designed to complement one another. One (the self-completion survey) provided mainly factual data on a very large number of visitors; the other (the personal interview survey) provided data in more depth — some factual, some concerned with feelings and attitudes — on a much smaller number. For practical reasons, the groups covered by the two surveys were different, one dealing with all visitors to the parks, the other only with people going into visitor centres.

But the broad approach in both cases was very similar. In particular both exercises took full account of the need for

- **representative samples** — which meant a careful choice of days when the research was to be carried out, and a method of selecting individuals which minimised the chance of bias creeping into the results;
- **good questionnaire design,** minimising the scope for misunderstanding; and
- **practical realism** — eg in designing self-completion 'leaflets' which recipients wouldn't reject as too complicated, in dropping questions visitors were unwilling to answer, and in keeping interviews to a length that wouldn't inconvenience visitors.

In both cases, the pilot exercise played an important part in modifying (and improving) original plans.

7

3. What the survey found

The study produced a wealth of statistical and other information on visitors to the two country parks. Some of the results may hold good for patterns of behaviour elsewhere (though without any similar studies in other country parks it is hard to tell); other findings are more likely to apply just to Rufford and Sherwood.

This chapter concentrates on those research findings which best illustrate what can — and cannot — be expected from an exercise of this kind.

Who the visitors are

Figures 1 and 2 present some of the key findings for the two parks taken together. (There were some differences between the parks which are discussed briefly on page 10.) Most of the information used for compiling these charts came from the self-completion survey, whose larger sample size made it much easier to analyse the various groups of visitors.

Figure 1 shows how old the visitors were, and how many came in the party. Adult visitors to the parks were predominantly aged between 25 and 44. There were far more visitors in this age-group than in the UK population as a whole. Similarly, there were fewer visitors aged 45 or over. But the visitors were by no means all families with children: just over half the groups visiting the parks brought no children with them, and the average group size is 3.2. In fact, slightly more visitors arrived in groups of two (32 per cent) than in groups of three (19 per cent) or four (25 per cent).

Figure 2 focusses on the visitors' social and employment status. The only question on the self-completion questionnaire which covered this was one which asked whether the members of the group were in or out of work. So some of the data for this chart has been taken from the much smaller personal interview survey, which dealt only with the activities of the head of the household concerned.

Taken together, the three sets of figures in the chart show that most visitors came from families where the head of the household was working, and usually in a professional, managerial or other non-manual job. A minority of around 15 per cent are retired. Meanwhile the proportion of unemployed is very small indeed at 2 per cent of heads of households, 5 per cent of adult visitors (less than half the national/regional average at the time of the survey).

Perhaps the most striking figure in the chart is the tiny 1 per cent of households headed by an unskilled manual worker — well below the national average of about 4½ per cent. It may be that unskilled workers (or members of their households) were less willing than others to take part in the personal interview survey; but it seems highly probable that unskilled manual workers are also much less likely to visit country parks in the first place.

Where the visitors came from

Visitors were asked to say which village or district they came from in the self-completion questionnaire. The information obtained from this question was then analysed three ways — by counties, by district council areas, and by distance from the park. In addition, the personal interview survey asked about the type of place visitors had set out from — eg whether it was their own home, or whether it was some form of holiday accommodation such as an hotel.

Figure 3 shows the results. Nearly two-thirds of the visitors came from Nottinghamshire, with the next two counties — South Yorkshire and Derbyshire — a long way behind. Although the two parks are fairly close to the Lincolnshire boundary, only a tiny proportion (2 per cent) of people came from that direction. Another 2 per cent came from overseas (most of these visitors went to Sherwood). A more detailed breakdown by district council

Figure 1: Who the visitors are: Age and composition of party

Source: Self-completion questionnaire.

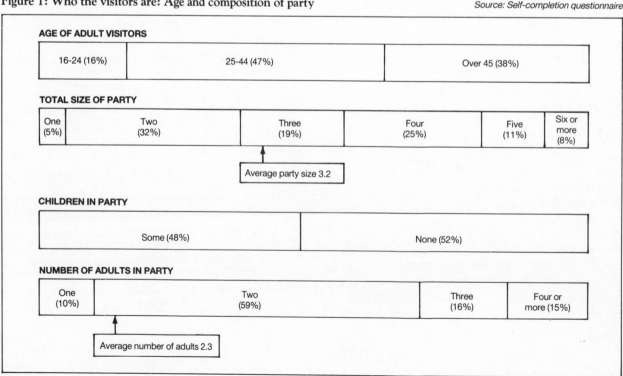

areas shows that it was the two districts closest to the parks — Mansfield and Newark — which provided the most visitors (roughly 15 per cent each). The city of Nottingham, 17 miles to the south, provided another 10 per cent, and Sheffield, 25 miles to the north, another 5 per cent. But the population of each of these two cities is several times greater than that of the district councils. So the parks appear to be less attractive to people from these cities than to people who live close by.

Figure 2: Who the visitors are: Social and employment status

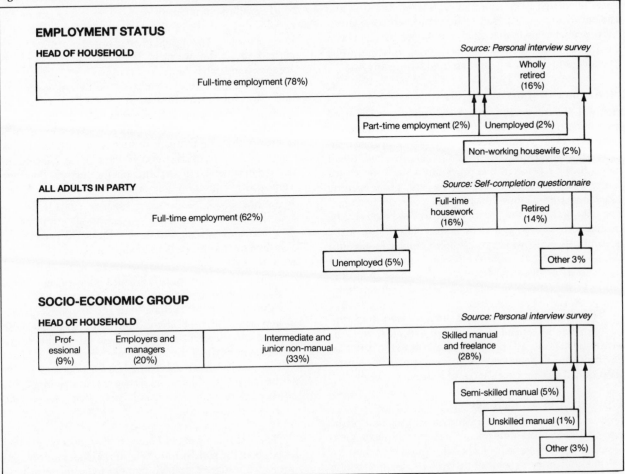

Figure 3: Where the visitors come from

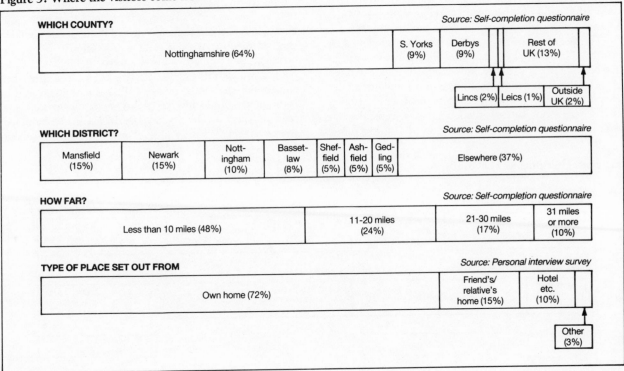

The strongly local appeal of the two parks is confirmed by the figures showing how far most people had come. Nearly half (48 per cent) of the visitors came from within a 10-mile radius — a line which includes Mansfield and Worksop, but stops well short of larger centres such as Nottingham and Sheffield; and only 10 per cent travelled 31 miles or more. The impression that the parks are mainly places people go to on short day trips is reinforced by the data on where people started out from: nearly three-quarters (72 per cent) came from home. Only 10 per cent had been staying away from home in holiday accommodation, while 15 per cent had been staying with friends or relatives.

First-timers versus old hands

Figure 4 presents some of the study's findings on visitors' trip-taking habits in general. The upper part of the chart shows how many visitors to Sherwood and Rufford had been there before: nearly three-quarters (74 per cent) had. But of these, only 57 per cent had previously visited the visitor centre as well as the outdoor part of the park. The remaining 17 per cent were visiting the visitor centre for the first time. The data on which this part of the chart was based is to be treated with caution as it came from replies to one of the questions — 5c — which people seem to have found difficult. Separate figures from the personal interview surveys (not shown in these charts) suggest that more than one-third (34 per cent) of visitors have been **at least ten times** before.

The bottom half of the chart summarises visitors' trip-taking habits in general. As might be expected, an overwhelming majority (83 per cent) of visitors to the park take day trips into the country at least once a month. Not far short of half (43 per cent) go out at least once a week.

How visitors decide to go

How did people make their decision to visit one of the parks? What outside influences — eg friends' recommendations, advertisements, guidebooks — prompted them?

Figure 5 presents some of the answers, using responses to the personal interview survey. It also draws from the one relevant question — on where people had heard or read about the parks in the previous six months — which appeared in the self-completion questionnaire.

The **decision to visit** one of the parks was usually taken by the respondent or his/her spouse. But it is interesting that in 8 per cent of cases, the decision was made by one or more of the children in the group. At Sherwood, children under 16 were particularly important decision-makers. The **timing** of the decision varied, though it was generally an impromptu one. Most (56 per cent) didn't decide to go until the day; of these 19 per cent hadn't even reached their decision by the time they left home. Another 22 per cent decided the previous day. Only a small minority (15 per cent) decided four days or more in advance. This percentage was higher at Sherwood than at Rufford — which is to be expected given the greater proportion of visitors who had come from outside the area.

The third and fourth parts of Figure 5 summarise people's replies to the open-ended questions in the personal interview survey about their main reasons for coming to the parks. Because the two parks' attractions differ, the results are shown separately here.

The reasons visitors gave were mostly rather generalised. Roughly a third in each park (29 per cent in Sherwood, 36 per cent in Rufford) just said they wanted an outing, without elaborating; another 14-15 per cent in each case were showing the park to friends or relatives; 10 per cent were simply 'passing through' and a further 5-8 per cent referred in general terms to bringing the children. But there were two more interesting findings:

- At Sherwood, 18 per cent came specifically for the Robin Hood associations. Not surprisingly, this interest was greatest among first-time visitors, 30 per cent of whom mentioned Robin Hood.
- At Rufford, 9 per cent said they had come to see the craft centre. But **not one person** is coded as having mentioned the visitor centre at Sherwood, with its Robin Hood exhibition. There may have been a coding problem here: it may simply have been too difficult to disentangle those who said they had come to Sherwood for the visitor centre from those who had come "for the Robin Hood associations" in general. Nonetheless it does suggest that the appeal of Sherwood is rooted in its intangible associations with the legend rather than any specific individual attraction.

The last three parts of **Figure 6** show how people had heard about the parks before their visit. Taken together, the three charts suggest that visitors are more likely to hear about the parks casually — eg from friends — than through formal channels such as advertisements or tourist information centres. Roughly two-thirds claimed that they "just always knew" about the parks or had heard about them by word of mouth; an even greater proportion (over three-quarters) said that they would never be influenced by publicity material such as posters or leaflets. But this conclusion needs to be treated with a pinch of salt, as it is by no means unusual for people to say that advertisements have no effect on their behaviour. It should also be noted that several of the ways visitors claimed to have heard about

Figure 4: First-timers or old hands?

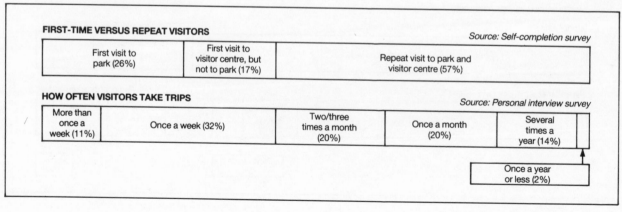

FIRST-TIME VERSUS REPEAT VISITORS			*Source: Self-completion survey*
First visit to park (26%)	First visit to visitor centre, but not to park (17%)	Repeat visit to park and visitor centre (57%)	

HOW OFTEN VISITORS TAKE TRIPS					*Source: Personal interview survey*
More than once a week (11%)	Once a week (32%)	Two/three times a month (20%)	Once a month (20%)	Several times a year (14%)	
				Once a year or less (2%)	

the parks in the previous six months — such as newspaper articles, newspaper ads, libraries, tourist information centres, guidebooks and TV and radio — were in fact direct or indirect results of Nottinghamshire's own marketing efforts.

One interesting finding from the "how did you first hear" question was the proportion of visitors who found out about the parks from signposts. Altogether, 13 per cent claimed that this was so. In fact, this figure masks a big difference between Sherwood and Rufford: at Sherwood, only 7 per cent said they had found out about the park from signposts, while at Rufford the figure was a remarkable 20 per cent. The Rufford figure is no doubt partly explained by the park's long frontage on the main A614; but it is still remarkably high.

What visitors do when they get there

The study covered three main aspects of what visitors do when they get to the parks:

- How long do they intend to stay?
- Do they go into visitor centres or do they stay outside?
- How much money do they spend?

Figure 6 presents a selection of the results.

The top part gives an idea of **how long visitors stay.** It is based on the self-completion questionnaire, which was designed for visitors to fill in as soon as they arrived. So it measures intentions, not actual stay. But the overwhelming proportion — 69 per cent — reckoned to stay at least an hour but not more than three hours. This finding was generally matched by the response to the personal interview survey, which was of course carried out later on in people's visits and so measured what they were actually doing as much as what they intended to do. The personal interview survey also showed that first-time visitors tend to stay a bit longer than repeat visitors; and (hardly surprisingly), visits in the autumn were generally a bit shorter than visits in the summer.

The second part of Figure 6 shows the proportion of visitors saying they were going to go into one of the parks' **visitor centres.** Over two-thirds (69 per cent) said they would when answering the self-completion questionnaire. A small proportion (8 per cent) hadn't made up their minds. Cross-tabulating people's answers to this question with some of their other answers on the questionnaire produced some interesting clues to people's reason for going to the centres. For example:

- Most of the visitors to the visitor centres are people who have been to the parks before. But the proportion of repeat visitors entering the centres is smaller than the proportion of repeat visitors to the parks as a whole. The minority of first-time visitors are much more likely than repeat visitors to go into the visitor centres.

- At Sherwood (but not Rufford) the visitor centre attracts a far greater proportion of parties with children than does the country park as a whole; equally, it attracts a smaller proportion of groups consisting entirely of adults. The Robin Hood exhibition which forms the centrepiece of the visitor centre is no doubt seen as more of an attraction for children than for adults. This conclusion doesn't appear to hold for the exhibition at Rufford, with its emphasis on high-quality crafts.

Figure 5: Deciding to visit the parks

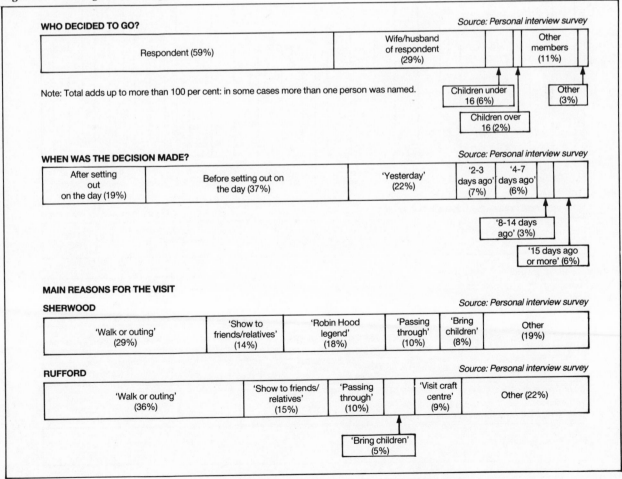

WHO DECIDED TO GO? — *Source: Personal interview survey*

| Respondent (59%) | Wife/husband of respondent (29%) | | Other members (11%) |

Note: Total adds up to more than 100 per cent: in some cases more than one person was named.

Children under 16 (6%)
Children over 16 (2%)
Other (3%)

WHEN WAS THE DECISION MADE? — *Source: Personal interview survey*

| After setting out on the day (19%) | Before setting out on the day (37%) | 'Yesterday' (22%) | '2-3 days ago' (7%) | '4-7 days ago' (6%) | |

'8-14 days ago' (3%)
'15 days ago or more' (6%)

MAIN REASONS FOR THE VISIT

SHERWOOD — *Source: Personal interview survey*

| 'Walk or outing' (29%) | 'Show to friends/relatives' (14%) | 'Robin Hood legend' (18%) | 'Passing through' (10%) | 'Bring children' (8%) | Other (19%) |

RUFFORD — *Source: Personal interview survey*

| 'Walk or outing' (36%) | 'Show to friends/relatives' (15%) | 'Passing through' (10%) | | 'Visit craft centre' (9%) | Other (22%) |

'Bring children' (5%)

The personal interview survey probed people's visits to the centres in greater depth — looking for example at the proportion of visitors going to different parts of each centre (eg exhibition, shop, café etc). These findings confirmed the attraction of the Robin Hood exhibitions to groups with children. Intriguingly, 8-9 per cent of people in each park claimed to have visited the visitor centre without having been to **any** of its component parts (perhaps the survey should have asked directly whether visitors had used the toilet facilities).

The bottom half of Figure 6 shows visitors' **spending patterns.** Roughly two-thirds (64 per cent) of visitors to the parks spent at least some money in the shop or café on each site; each group that did spend money spent an average of about £3.50. As there was an average of slightly over three people per group, this implies spending of just over £1 per head. More people spent below this amount than spent more: the average figure will have been disproportionately influenced by the small proportion of people spending large amounts of money (many items in the Rufford Craft Centre, for example, cost more than £10).

Figure 6: What visitors do

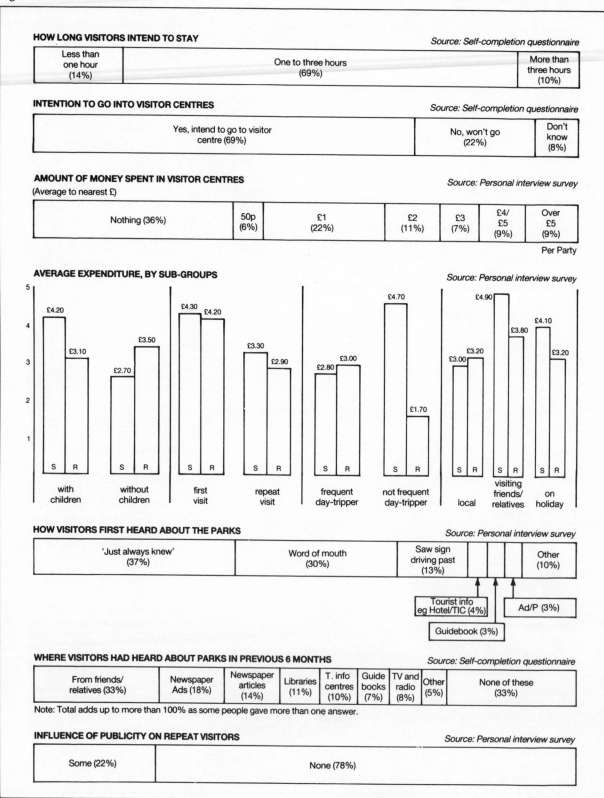

Some of the most interesting findings from the whole survey are shown at the bottom of Figure 6. This shows how much different **types** of party spent in the two parks' visitor centres. Average expenditure per party was roughly the same in each park (£3.80 at Sherwood, £3.30 at Rufford). But the detailed pattern varied considerably so findings for the two parks have been presented separately.

The small charts show in particular that

- **Parties with children** spend more at Sherwood than parties without children. This echoes the greater popularity of the Robin Hood exhibition with groups including children (see p11): the Robin Hood (and other) items on sale in the shop, and the offerings at the outdoor cafe, were clearly more popular with them too. At Rufford, whether groups came with or without children didn't appear to make much difference.

- In both parks, **first-time visitors** spent considerably (at least £1) more than **repeat visitors**. Visitors weren't asked to break down their spending according to where it took place (eg between shops and cafés), but responses to the question on where visitors had been within the visitor centres (see Appendix B, question 5) showed that first-time visitors were more likely to go to the souvenir and craft shops, but not to the cafés. So it is presumably in the shops that they spend their extra money.

- Spending by **visitors who take regular day trips** (defined as at least two or three a month) and those who don't shows some very odd variations. At Sherwood, regular day-trippers spend much more than the rest; at Rufford it's the other way round (£1.70 against £3.00). Despite the limited size of the personal interview survey, big differences like this are very unlikely to be a fluke.

More research would be needed to establish the reasons. It may simply be that the high-quality crafts on sale at Rufford have a greater appeal to the types of people who take lots of day trips; while the main items on sale at Sherwood (many of which might be classed as souvenirs rather than crafts) are more popular with the types of people who don't go out very much. Could it be that 'old hands' splash out only when they see something really special?

- In both parks, **people who are visiting friends and relatives** are likely to spend more money than those who live locally or who are on holiday. Again the reasons for this are a bit mysterious, and more research would be needed to find out why this difference arises.

What visitors think

One of the general aims of the study was to identify what visitors thought about the parks: which bits they liked, which they didn't like, and what improvements they would like to see. An attempt was also made to assess whether visitors' experiences of the parks were in line with what they expected.

In general, people's reactions to the parks, as measured by the personal interview survey, were very favourable indeed. All found it much easier to identify things they liked about the parks than things they disliked. For example, people liked

- the walks (33 per cent at Sherwood, 27 per cent at Rufford);
- trees/the forest (26 per cent at Sherwood, 10 per cent at Rufford);
- peace and quiet (20 per cent at Sherwood, 15 per cent at Rufford), and

- unspoilt natural character (19 per cent at Sherwood, 25 per cent at Rufford).

Only 2-3 per cent were unable to identify anything they liked. With **dislikes,** the opposite was true, with many people (50 per cent at Sherwood, 55 per cent at Rufford) unable to think of anything they disliked at all. The only criticisms were raised by a small minority. For example:

- Too organised/formal (7 per cent at Sherwood).
- Café too exposed (7 per cent at Sherwood).
- Inadequate car parking (7 per cent at Rufford).

Similarly, visitors' response to the open-ended question on the self-completion questionnaire about possible improvements was very muted. Car parking at Rufford (raised by 8 per cent of respondents) was the most widely mentioned; other favourites included children's adventure playgrounds, more toilets and more seats, though none of these was mentioned by more than 5 per cent. The only individual item that was raised as a separate question was signposting (see Appendix B, question 2). Roughly a quarter in each park (27 per cent at Sherwood, 21 per cent at Rufford) thought it was inadequate.

This story of general satisfaction with the parks was confirmed yet again with the 'agree/disagree' statements read out during the personal interview survey (see Appendix B, question 22). Visitors unerringly agreed with all the positive statements, and disagreed with all the negative ones. The nearest they came to overturning this principle was with the statement

"Sherwood Forest is a place to get away from large numbers of people"

with which 37 per cent — a substantial proportion, but still a minority — disagreed.

More interesting were visitor reactions to different parts of the visitor centres. These are shown in the first part of **Figure 7.** Again, the general reaction was very favourable — in only one of the eight cases (the café at Sherwood) did the "liked a lot" percentage fall below half. But at Rufford it was the café which got the best rating.

The bottom half of Figure 7 shows how first-time visitors' experiences of the parks compared with their expectations. The personal interview survey found that people's expectations were only very hazily defined, so the figures should be treated with caution. But they confirm, yet again, visitors' overwhelmingly favourable view of the parks. At Sherwood, a **majority** (57 per cent) of these turned out to have found the park better than they thought, and only a tiny minority worse. Rufford produced fewer surprises, with 60 per cent finding it in line with their expectations; but again, virtually all the remaining 40 per cent thought it was better.

The reasons behind people's 'better/worse' response were then probed by asking them **in what way** the parks differed from what they expected. The answers are summarised at the bottom of Figure 7. Roughly a third (30 per cent) were surprised to find Sherwood so organised and developed, and another 8 per cent thought it more commercial. The same tendencies arose at Rufford, though they were less pronounced: also important here was visitors' perception of the size of the park, which 8 per cent had expected to be smaller.

Figure 7: What visitors think

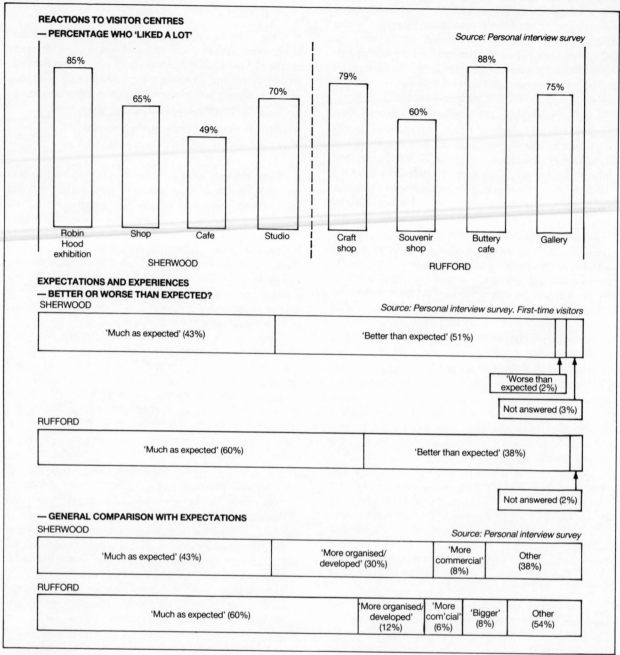

REACTIONS TO VISITOR CENTRES
— PERCENTAGE WHO 'LIKED A LOT'

Source: Personal interview survey

SHERWOOD: Robin Hood exhibition 85%, Shop 65%, Cafe 49%, Studio 70%

RUFFORD: Craft shop 79%, Souvenir shop 60%, Buttery cafe 88%, Gallery 75%

EXPECTATIONS AND EXPERIENCES
— BETTER OR WORSE THAN EXPECTED?

SHERWOOD — *Source: Personal interview survey. First-time visitors*
'Much as expected' (43%) | 'Better than expected' (51%) | 'Worse than expected (2%) | Not answered (3%)

RUFFORD
'Much as expected' (60%) | 'Better than expected' (38%) | Not answered (2%)

— GENERAL COMPARISON WITH EXPECTATIONS

SHERWOOD — *Source: Personal interview survey*
'Much as expected' (43%) | 'More organised/developed' (30%) | 'More commercial' (8%) | Other (38%)

RUFFORD
'Much as expected' (60%) | 'More organised/developed' (12%) | 'More com'cial' (6%) | 'Bigger' (8%) | Other (54%)

Conclusion

To try to describe a 'typical' visitor to one of the parks is tempting providence, as the study showed that a wide variety of people visit them for a variety of motives. But seven things stand out in particular, not all of them what might be expected:

- The parks are relatively popular with young-to-middle aged adults, slightly less so with older people.

- Most people came in smallish, family-sized groups. But only about half of these groups include any children under 16.

- Visitors are overwhelmingly from households headed by people in professional, managerial or other non-manual jobs. Hardly any come from unskilled manual backgrounds.

- Most visitors live very locally — within 30 miles — and make their decision to visit the parks in a very casual way, either the day before or on the day they set out. Reasons for going are seldom very specific.

- Even if special allowance is made for people's apparent unwillingness to admit that they are influenced by advertising, casual word of mouth — or even just 'common knowledge' — is a far more important source of information about the parks than the various formal channels.

- Most visitors like what they know of the parks, even though some found Sherwood Forest rather busy and developed. But few had thought much about other ways in which the parks might be developed, even at the level of basic physical facilities such as catering, car parking and toilets.

- Signposting is remarkably important. No less than 20 per cent first found out about Rufford from the signpost outside. But a substantial minority — roughly a quarter — felt that it wasn't adequate.

The next chapter discusses some of the implications of these findings for Nottinghamshire's management and promotion of the parks.

4. Using the results

The consultants' report on the Sherwood/Rufford study was presented in August 1983. This was not of course the end of the County Council's involvement: on the contrary, completion of the report was where the Council's real work began. The Council has been using the study's findings in three main ways:

- as a guide to **promotional strategy;**
- as a **management tool;** and
- as a **guide to future research.**

But it is only fair to record that some of the results have been used very little, if at all. Some of the reasons for this were purely due to outside events; but some were due to the design and management of the survey, and bear some useful messages for future research of this kind.

Promotional strategy

The original aim of the project was to provide the kind of management information Nottinghamshire needed to put its 'marketing approach' for country parks into effect — see page 3. This emphasis changed while the study was in progress, but the results nonetheless had some important implications for the way the County Council handled its publicity. For example:

- The study showed that first-time visitors (many of whom were tourists from outside the area) spent more in the parks than repeat visitors. As a result **promotional activity aimed at tourists** — both that handled by the County itself and that channelled through the East Midlands Tourist Board — has been increased.
- The study found that, of the various forms of publicity, **newspaper coverage** has most impact. So the County has — successfully — pursued a greater amount of press reporting on its country parks.
- **Signposting** was considered inadequate by roughly a quarter of the parks' visitors — see page 13 — despite its apparent importance as a means of attracting visitors to the parks. Possible improvements are now being investigated.
- Roughly a fifth of first-time visitors to Rufford expected the park to be smaller than it is (see p13). This misconception is being tackled in the County's promotional material, which emphasises the park's **size and range of landscapes,** including the lake.
- Some sectors of the population who turned out to be poorly represented in the **visitor profiles** (eg unskilled manual workers) are now being made the target of a specific scheme, the aim of which is to encourage and enable such groups to visit the countryside.

Management

So far most of the impact of the study has been at the level of general management philosophy and undertaking rather than detailed policy. But even at this level, the survey's findings have had important results: some considerable changes have already been made which will have implications for any future investment. For example, in visitor centres, it is clear that exhibitions need to be changed regularly if the repeat visitors — who make up a big majority of all the visitors to the parks — are to be drawn inside. A responsibility also rests on park rangers, who are becoming more visitor- and less land-management oriented. In particular, they can attract many more repeat visitors by organising — and participating in — events such as guided walks, puppet shows, and nature study.

It is also clear that neither of the extreme views about management of country parks — that they must be absolutely quiet all the time, or that they must support a ceaseless round of jollity — can be justified by visitors' attitudes. Most value the peace and quiet the parks provide, but few deny that events have an important role to play, especially those that attract children, and few seem to have been put off by the organised, developed nature of parts of Sherwood Forest.

The study has also helped to get rid of some misconceptions, particularly about the importance and attractions of Sherwood Forest. Setting aside the small minority of people on holiday (many of whom are visiting the park for the first time) it becomes clear that in some senses — despite some very obvious physical distinctions — Sherwood isn't very different from Rufford or, for that matter, many other country parks. Most people are local, and just want a quiet, easy day out. This suggests, for example, that it is probably not worthwhile setting the park up to cater for people who have come on long day trips.

Further research

Since the Sherwood/Rufford study was completed, its findings have acted as a springboard for several smaller-scale research projects. These have included:

- Studies of passengers using a special (Sherwood Forester) bus network in 1982 and 1983, through interviews and self-completion questionnaires.
- Studies of people taking part in events — and of those not taking part — at Sherwood Forest Visitor Centre in 1982 and 1983, again through interviews and self-completion questionnaires.
- A series of group discussions on the barriers that prevent low income and unemployed families from visiting the countryside.
- A series of street interviews in the Nottingham area finding out about people's awareness of Nottinghamshire's country parks.
- A survey of signposting of tourist attractions, which is being carried out by Survey Research Associates as part of an experiment under the auspices of the English Tourist Board. This involves comparisons of visitor behaviour before and after installation of selected signposts.
- A survey of tourists (as opposed to day trippers) visiting the Sherwood Forest area. The field work is being undertaken at Sherwood Forest Visitor Centre and includes the 'before' element of monitoring the English Tourist Board's signposting experiment.

More generally, the data collected for the study will form an invaluable base against which future trends can be measured. This should make it very much easier to measure the effect of new developments such as improved facilities and changes in the way the parks are promoted. To do this, the County now intends to continue the main elements of the survey on a regular basis; at the same time, it plans to extend its research to cover two of its other parks, Creswell Crags and Leen Valley.

Shortcomings of the study

Important though all this progress has been, there have been several obstacles to using the results as much as was hoped. Some have resulted from policy changes: the change in the County Council's marketing strategy, and the corresponding cut in the publicity budget while the survey was in progress reduced the relevance of parts of the research. But some of the limitations to the usefulness of the study directly reflected its conception, design and management.

In particular:

- **There was too much information too late.** It took two years from the original pilot exercise in August 1981 to the presentation of the finished report in August 1983. The report itself ran to 109 A4-sized pages plus 51 tables — making it an invaluable source of detail but obscuring many of the key findings.

    This problem was not necessarily the fault of the agency which carried out the research. With the benefit of hindsight, it is clear that these points should have been dealt with in the specifications. For example, the specification should have been more explicit about the length and type of write-up that was required. Meanwhile the balance between fieldwork and analysis probably wasn't quite right: it would have been better to put fewer resources into fieldwork and more into analysis. There was certainly more data generated than could easily be handled.

- **County Council staff haven't yet had enough experience using this kind of information.** The 'cultural change' required to get administrators to use detailed survey information was probably underestimated. This reinforces the need for adequate resources for analysing the data and for a simple, clear and timely presentation of the main findings.

- **There was nothing to compare the data with.** It may be interesting to know that, for example, 69 per cent of visitors to Sherwood and Rufford stay between one and three hours; but without any basis for comparison, it is hard to make much use of this finding. Norms or other quantified objectives, similar figures for other country parks or even past figures for Sherwood and Rufford would all have helped. Now that the Sherwood/Rufford data has been gathered, this will of course make future data — both here and elsewhere — much easier to interpret and use, as noted above.

5. Some general lessons

Some parts of the Sherwood/Rufford survey worked very well, others less so. This chapter considers the strengths and weaknesses of the research, and draws some lessons for future studies of this kind. Some suggestions for further reading are given at the end.

Objectives of the study

The initial objectives of the Sherwood/Rufford study were clearly articulated, as outlined on p3. These objectives had to be changed following a shift in the Council's marketing policy (see p15), but their mere existence was a great help throughout the design and execution of the fieldwork.

All this may sound a bit obvious. But the fact remains that there is very little point in setting up a visitor survey simply to satisfy general curiosity. The starting point in most cases should be a set of strategic objectives for the site covering, for example, its management, conservation and promotion to the general public. The next step is to identify from these which points a survey will help to clarify. In turn, this requires a clear idea of how the findings of the survey are going to be used to guide future policy and practice.

It may be helpful to set out the objectives of the survey as a series of questions, with some linked 'multiple choice' answers. For example.

Who are the visitors?

If mostly groups without children — review need to spend money on adventure playgrounds programme.
If mainly elderly people — consider spending extra money on seats/path resurfacing.

How do visitors decide to come?

If spur of the moment decision — concentrate promotional resources on radio campaigns, for example.
If signposting important — improve it.

What do visitors do?

If some areas under-visited — review management/ signposting/spending on facilities.
If most visitors stay at least three hours — improve range and quality of catering.

Which visitors spend most in visitor centres?

If repeat visitors — encourage them to come back by organising special events, changing exhibitions etc.
If first-time visitors from outside the area — concentrate publicity on tourist offices, guidebook entries etc.
If mainly local visitors — encourage them to come through local publicity such as ads and articles in local newspapers.

At the same time, it's important not to be too ambitious. Experience with the personal interview survey at Sherwood/Rufford shows that it is particularly difficult to measure visitors' **expectations, motivation** and **attitudes** in an exercise of this kind. For example, questions 12a to 12d of the personal interview survey (see Appendix B) sought information about visitors' expectations of the parks, and how these compared with what they actually found; but many of the answers were vague and generalised, and people clearly had difficulty answering the questions.

Getting the survey work done

There are two main choices — doing the work in-house, using existing staff; and contracting the work out to an agency.

Using existing staff can be economical, especially where the tasks are simple and easy to define — eg handing out a self-completion questionnaire, recording the number handed out, and getting people to place completed questionnaires in boxes provided. But some tasks are much more complicated, and demand a good deal more experience. This applies particularly to personal interviews: however simple the pre-prepared questions may sound, reading them out in a way that avoids implying that a particular reply is expected, and listening to and coding the answers all requires a measure of experience regular staff may not possess.

Three other considerations argue in favour of contracting the work to an outside body:

- **Detailed supervision.** Even very simple tasks require close coordination and supervision: the smallest of errors repeated many times over can easily invalidate the whole exercise. It is often much safer to get someone to supervise the work who has some experience of what can go wrong.

- **Staff numbers.** Many surveys require a large number of staff to be available on a particular day — though quite possibly just for that day. Most market research agencies have easy access to part-time workers who can turn out as required; it is much more difficult to arrange for a large number of in-house staff to be free. Nor is it good enough simply to work out which days the staff concerned can be made available once holidays, meetings and other commitments have been totted up: often the choice of day will depend on the sample design for the survey as a whole.

- **Prompt reporting.** A deadline for the submission of the final report should, of course, be written into the work specification sent out to interested bodies. It thus forms part of the contract. This financial incentive makes it much easier to get the report submitted on time with an outside agency than with an in-house group.

If in-house staff can be spared, without any additional cost such as overtime payments, this can of course work out cheaper. But if time is wasted, or if mistakes are made, the saving will be more apparent than real. At the same time, the cost of employing professional interviewers should not be exaggerated. The following approximate figures are based on data supplied by two major market research companies in mid-1984:

Cost of employing a professional interviewer for a day	£20
Supervision and general overheads, per interviewer per day	£20
Cost of associated questionnaire design, analysis and report preparation, per interviewer per day	£20
Total daily cost of interviewing, including supervision, project design, analysis and report preparation	£60

These figures will naturally vary according to project — the last of them most of all, as a simple but very large survey will cost a lot less to organise, on a per-interviewer-per-day basis, than a small but very complicated one. But the sums give a rough idea nonetheless. For example they indicate that a modest three-day site survey conducted by five interviewers would cost about

$$3 \times 5 \times £60 = £900$$

It may be possible to save a bit by getting some — if not all — of the work done by in-house staff. In the Sherwood/Rufford survey it was decided at the outset that trained staff were not needed to hand out the self-completion leaflets to drivers who entered the parks, and the job was done by County Council employees plus some specially-recruited temporary staff. The same was true of the people who acted as counters to monitor the flow of visitors through the visitor centres on the day the personal interview surveys were carried out. In the event, there were some administrative problems with the use of County Council staff, and there were some survey days when visitors weren't properly counted. In principle, in-house staff should be perfectly able to deal with simpler tasks of this kind — provided they are given clear instructions and are properly trained; but to judge from Sherwood/Rufford at least, it can be risky to assume there will be enough people available at the right time.

An alternative 'hybrid' approach would be to contract the fieldwork out to a market research company, but to do some of the analysis in-house. In particular, it may be possible to use some of the computer and staff resources of local authority Treasurers' departments — especially if there is spare capacity during a quiet season of the year. However, this could easily negate the prompt reporting advantage of using a contractor.

Choosing a research technique

The simplest technique of all is to count how many visitors do particular things and when they do them. A simple analysis of visitor flows may, for example, be all that is needed to gauge the adequacy of car parking arrangements, or the hours when catering facilities or visitor centres should be open. In principle, it ought to be possible to carry out such an analysis using mechanical counters, though experience with these in the early stages of the Sherwood/Rufford survey was not encouraging.

Anything which goes beyond simple measurements of visitor flows is bound to involve asking visitors questions — which in turn means some kind of questionnaire. The Sherwood/Rufford survey illustrated the benefits and pitfalls of the two main options — questionnaires visitors fill in themselves, and questionnaires which are used as the basis of personal interviews.

The **self-completion questionnaire** was on the whole very successful. The sample of 6,800 completed questionnaires — representing nearly 16,000 adult visitors altogether — was big enough to allow a wide range of analyses, eg dividing the totals up according to age groups, days of the week when the visit took place, where people lived, first-time versus repeat visitors, and whether visitors went to the visitor centres or not. From these a very clear picture of the flow of visitors to the parks was obtained.

Meanwhile the **personal interview survey** proved to have several limitations. Most obvious was the **basis** of the sample. As the survey covered only those visitors who passed through visitor centres, the results may well have been biased: visitors who do not go to the centres may have quite different attitudes and behave quite differently. And the size of the sample limited the usefulness of the results. The survey was based on 624 interviews — a little over 300 in each park. This meant that it was difficult to make

detailed comparisons between sub-groups. It nonetheless provided some useful insights into areas the self-completion questionnaire was unable to penetrate. This was true especially of

- visitors' initial awareness of the parks as places to visit;
- the influence of promotions on the decision to visit;
- how the decision was made to visit, and who made it;
- general likes and dislikes about the parks; and
- expenditure within the parks.

All the same, as noted on p13, the answers to some questions — particularly those dealing with expectations and attitudes — were disappointing. Although it's possible to ask some more complicated and searching questions in a personal interview than in a self-completion questionnaire, there are evidently strict limits on how ambitious those questions can be. But the personal interview surveys cost vastly more. The figures aren't directly comparable because the dates and time periods chosen for each exercise differed, but the following table gives a rough impression.

	Self-completion questionnaire	Personal interview survey
Total number of questionnaires completed	6800	624
Number of days	12	9
Number of interviewers	7	5
Average questionnaires completed per interviewer per day	81	14

In other words, each interviewer managed to get roughly six times as many self-completion questionnaires filled in per day as personal interview surveys. On the basis of the above figures, if it costs £60 a day to keep an interviewer in the field (see p17 above), each self-completion questionnaire would cost about 75p, and each personal interview survey about £4.25.

Given the extra cost involved, and the limits to the amount of extra information that can be obtained, personal interview surveys are likely to be useful only where data on visitors' backgrounds is particularly important. This applies especially to the questions on occupation and social class, on which the self-completion questionnaires produced little useful information.

Practicalities

One useful measure of the success (or otherwise) of the survey methods used is visitors' **response rates.** The Sherwood/Rufford results are shown in **Figure 8.** With both the self-completion and personal interview exercises, useful responses were obtained from between half and two-thirds of the initial contacts made (55 per cent with the self-completion survey, 67 per cent with the personal interviews). With each survey, the response was reduced by

- **Non-eligibility** — eg because the visitor had been contacted before; and
- **Refusals.** In percentage terms, this was much less of a problem with the self-completion survey than the personal interview survey — it's much more difficult to refuse a leaflet which is being thrust at you than to turn away an interviewer. But there were no doubt plenty of people who accepted leaflets without the least intention

of filling them in, a fact which is reflected in the sizeable proportion of leaflets given out but not returned, or returned incomplete.

With the self-completion questionnaire, the response was also reduced a little by the number of cars which were missed: there were some circumstances when it simply wasn't possible for interviewers to give out questionnaires to everyone, especially in busy periods. Reasons included:

- Cars overtaking while questionnaires were being handed out.

- A traffic diversion round a large traffic island.
- Interviewers unexpectedly running out of questionnaires.

A further gap in the coverage of the self-completion questionnaire — not revealed by Figure 8 — arose because of the need to leave coach parties out of the survey. In the early stages, attempts were made to include coach parties, by giving drivers special questionnaires to give out to their passengers; but this proved to be very time-consuming, and many coach drivers refused to take part.

Figure 8: Visitors' response to the survey

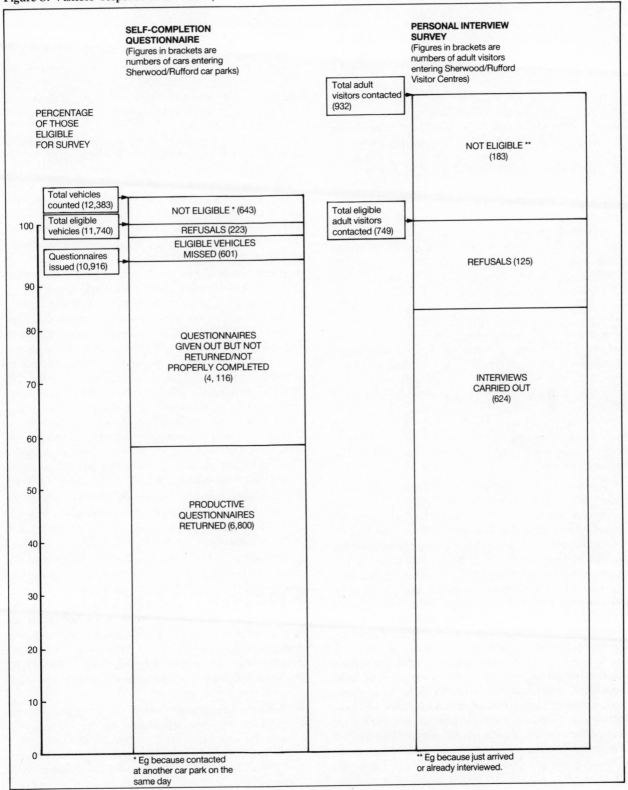

Despite these gaps, the response rates from the two exercises were considered highly respectable for a survey of this kind. They could easily have been much lower. As it was, the pilot survey turned out to be extremely important in each case — by establishing, for example, that visitors were much more likely to fill in the self-completion leaflets if they were prompted to do so straight away — and that there was much more resistance to interviews of 20-25 minutes than to 15-minute ones.

These findings underline very firmly indeed the need for a **pilot survey,** which can be used both as a learning process for the staff concerned and as a test-bed for the methods to be used. The investment of time will amply repay itself. It's important to leave enough time between the pilot exercise and the main fieldwork for any necessary modifications to sampling methods, questionnaire design etc to be made.

Experience with the Sherwood/Rufford survey also confirmed how important it is to get the nuts-and-bolts right — however trivial these may seem. The interviewer who runs out of questionnaires (or even of pencils) may well upset the balance of the sample, so biasing the conclusions. Some minor pieces of hardware — such as special armbands or badges for interviewers — may have a big impact on people's reactions. And things like collecting boxes need to be carefully sited, properly marked and regularly emptied.

Questionnaire design

The two Sherwood/Rufford questionnaires are reproduced at Appendices A and B. Both worked reasonably well — though the pilot exercise in each case was an essential step in the design of a successful questionnaire.

Even so, one interesting problem arose with the self-completion questionnaire (Appendix A). This was with questions 5a to 5f which asked for information about individual adult visitors (as opposed to the car driver or the group as a whole). Although this was redesigned and simplified after the first phase of the fieldwork, it still didn't work as well as was hoped, as some people were confused by the grid which allowed one column for each adult. Even so, the proportion failing to answer this part of the questionnaire properly was never higher than 15 per cent.

Although not really a 'problem' with the method, the question on where people came from (question 1) could have been phrased to produce more useful information. The wording used was

"Where did you set out from on your journey here today? Please write name of town and district, or village."

The information which came from this question wasn't as precise as might have been expected. Replies such as 'Nottingham' weren't really detailed enough to allow for a detailed breakdown of how far people had come; in the event it was necessary to analyse this data by grouping places of origin according to district council boundaries. A finer network of places, covering villages and neighbourhoods within cities, would have been more appropriate.

The general message is that questionnaires cannot be too simple. Any question which can be misunderstood will be, by a few people at least. Even the most innocuous question can sometimes be read two ways. With self-completion questionnaires at least, it's important to avoid complicated-looking grids and codes, and to add instructions wherever people might not be absolutely clear about what's wanted. Watch out, too, for questions that are worded in a way that implies a particular answer is expected.

Sampling design

There are two main decisions to make with surveys of this kind:

- when to do the work
- which people to contact

Both the Sherwood/Rufford exercises were carried out on days carefully chosen to represent a 'mix' of seasons of the year, and times when special events were or were not arranged; the self-completion survey also covered selected weekdays as well as weekends. All the personal interview surveys were carried out over three-day long weekends, covering Friday, Saturday and Sunday.

With both surveys, schemes were designed to sample a representative selection of visitors on the days chosen. As things turned out, the scheme devised for the self-completion survey wasn't necessary, as it proved possible to give the leaflets to everyone. But with the personal inverviews, it took a lot of care — and some experiment in the field — to design a sampling scheme that was practical as well as representative.

In general, it's worth devoting considerable resources to devising a sampling scheme which makes sense. If the sample taken isn't representative, you can't expect to rely on the conclusions reached. In selecting days for the work, it may be difficult to test sampling methods in the field (though simple visitor counts on selected days of the week and seasons of the year may act as a guide); but it's essential to test methods of sampling individual visitors. Some options worth considering include

- **Random sampling** — eg selecting only these cars with a 5 as the last digit of the number plate. The approach used with the personal interview survey — stopping the first visitor to pass through the visitor centre after the completion of the previous interview — was a kind of random sample, but this might not always work, eg at a site where some visitors on guided tours pass through at regular intervals.

- **Quota sampling** — which usually involves pre-selecting set proportions of people of particular types to interview (eg families with at least two children; elderly couples with both partners assumed to be over 65; young couples between 20 and 30 etc). To do this normally requires some kind of preliminary survey to establish in what proportion the visitors come.

- A **complete census** — ie covering everyone, as with the self-completion survey. There's no particular advantage in sampling if it's genuinely possible to cover everyone. But it's still a good idea to have contingency sampling arrangements just in case crowds intensify.

Further reading

Recreation site survey manual: Methods and techniques for conducting visitor surveys,
Tourism and Recreation Research Unit, Edinburgh, Countryside Commission for Scotland, 1983.

Marketing for nonprofit organisations,
Philip Kotler, Prentice-Hall, second edition, 1982.

Tourism marketing for small business,
Malcolm Wood (compiler and editor), English Tourist Board, 1980.

Appendix A: Self-completion questionnaire

Nottinghamshire County Council

Leisure Services Department

VISITORS SURVEY

* Please help us to improve the Park for visitors by completing this leaflet now, before you leave the car park.

* Just give your answers by putting a tick (√) in the appropriate boxes or by writing in where appropriate. (If you have nothing to write with – the interviewer has some spare pens).

* Then put the completed leaflet in any of the Collecting Bins provided. Thank you.

Help us to help you...

Another way of returning this leaflet is by posting it (no stamp needed) to:

Leisure Services (Countryside)
Notts. County Council
FREEPOST
Nottingham
NG2 1BR

FOR OFFICE USE ONLY   P.662

CAR Questionnaire, RUFFORD (135-6 Spare)

(137)		(138)
2		Car Park
Rufford		(139-40)

Date: Sat 16th Jan   04
        Sun 14th Feb   05

'Serial No.   (141-144)

Time   (145-148)

---

6. How long do you plan to stay here in the Park today?   (132)

PLEASE TICK
ONE BOX ONLY

   Less than 1 hour   [ ] 1
   1-3 hours   [ ] 2
   More than 3 hours   [ ] 3

7. Are you likely to go to the Craft Centre on this visit?   (133)

   Yes   [ ] 1
   No   [ ] 2
   Don't know   [ ] 3

8. Are there any improvements you would like to see, or anything that you would like provided for visitors here at the Park? *PLEASE WRITE IN*

9. Have you visited any of the following parks during the last four weeks?

Please tick any boxes that apply

      VISITED IN LAST 4 WEEKS (134)

   Sherwood Forest Country Park   [ ] 1
   Thoresby Hall   [ ] 2
   Clumber Park   [ ] 3
   Creswell Crags   [ ] 4
   Newstead Abbey   [ ] 5
   None of the above   [ ] 6

THANK YOU FOR YOUR HELP. PLEASE PUT THIS LEAFLET IN ANY OF THE COLLECTION BINS.

21

1. Where did you set out from on your journey here today? *PLEASE WRITE NAME OF TOWN & DISTRICT, OR VILLAGE*

_____ (101-102)

2. Did you find the signposting adequate on your way to the Park? (103)

Please tick one box

Yes [ ]1
No [ ]2

3. During the past 6 months or so, have you read or heard about Rufford in any of the following ways? (104)

Please tick all boxes that apply

Newspaper advertisements [✓]1
Newspaper articles [ ]2
Radio features [ ]3
TV features [ ]4

(105)
Tourist Information Centres [ ]1
Libraries [ ]2
Hotels [ ]3
Guidebooks [ ]4
From friends/relatives [ ]5
Other *(PLEASE DESCRIBE)* [ ]6
_____

No, none of the above [ ]7

4.a Including yourself, how many people have come in the car to the Park today?

PLEASE WRITE NUMBER IN BOX → (106) [ ]

b And how many of them are adult, that is aged 16 or over?

PLEASE WRITE NUMBER IN BOX → (107) [ ]

PLEASE TICK APPROPRIATE BOXES TO SHOW THE ANSWER FOR YOURSELF & FOR EACH OTHER ADULT IN THE CAR.

	YOU	OTHER ADULTS FIRST	SECOND	THIRD
5.a Please tick box to show whether male or female:	(108)	(114)	(120)	(126)
Male	[✓]1	[✓]1	[✓]1	[✓]1
Female	[ ]2	[ ]2	[ ]2	[ ]2
b Please tick box to show your (and each other adult's) age group:	(109)	(115)	(121)	(127)
16-24	[ ]1	[ ]1	[ ]1	[ ]1
25-44	[ ]2	[ ]2	[ ]2	[ ]2
45+	[ ]3	[ ]3	[ ]3	[ ]3
c Have you (and has each other adult) visited this Park before?	(110)	(116)	(122)	(128)
Yes	[ ]1	[ ]1	[ ]1	[ ]1
No	[ ]2	[ ]2	[ ]2	[ ]2
d Have you (and has each other adult) been to the Rufford Craft Centre on a previous visit?	(111)	(117)	(123)	(129)
Yes	[ ]1	[ ]1	[ ]1	[ ]1
No	[ ]2	[ ]2	[ ]2	[ ]2
e Which of the following applies to you (and to each other adult)?	(112)	(118)	(124)	(130)
Paid job, full or part-time	[ ]1	[ ]1	[ ]1	[ ]1
No paid job at present/Unemployed	[ ]2	[ ]2	[ ]2	[ ]2
Retired	[ ]3	[ ]3	[ ]3	[ ]3
Full-time housework	[ ]4	[ ]4	[ ]4	[ ]4
Other	[ ]5	[ ]5	[ ]5	[ ]5
f Whereabouts do you (and each other adult) live?	(113)	(119)	(125)	(131)
Notts./Derbys./Leics./S. Yorks/W. Lincs	[ ]1	[ ]1	[ ]1	[ ]1
Elsewhere in the UK	[ ]2	[ ]2	[ ]2	[ ]2
Outside the UK *(Please state country)*	[ ]3	[ ]3	[ ]3	[ ]3

PLEASE TURN OVER

22

Appendix B: Personal interview survey questionnaire

SHERWOOD

scpr
The institute for social surveys

SURVEY RESEARCH CENTRE
Head Office: 35 Northampton Square London EC1 0AX   Tel: 01-250 1866
Northern Field Office: Charazel House Gainford Darlington Co. Durham DL2 3EG   Tel: 032 576 888

P.662   Survey of Visitors to Sherwood & Rufford   August 1982

Serial No [ ][ ][ ]   SHERWOOD [1]
(101-103)   (104)

We are carrying out a survey for Nottinghamshire County Council about the visitors who come here and what they do on their visit so that the Council can provide the facilities people want.

		Col./Code	Skip to
	TIME INTERVIEW STARTED : _____		
1.	First of all, whereabouts did your journey start from on your visit here today ? WRITE NAME OF TOWN/VILLAGE _____		
2.	Did you set out on the journey today from your own home or from a friend's/relative's home or from somewhere else ? PROBE IF NECESSARY Own home Friend's/relative's home Holiday base (eg hotel) Other (SPECIFY) _____	(105) 1 2 3 4	
3.	What was the main form of transport that you used to get here ? PROBE IF NECESSARY *ONE CODE ONLY. IF MORE THAN ONE MENTIONED, PROBE FOR MAIN TYPE* Car/van/minibus Public transport bus Private hired coach Motorcycle Bicycle On foot Other (SPECIFY) _____	(106) 1 2 3 4 5 6 7	
4.	By the time you leave, how long altogether do you expect that your visit in the Park will have lasted ? *ONE CODE ONLY* Up to ½ hour More than ½ hr - 1 hour More than 1 hr - 2 hours More than 2 hrs - 4 hours More than 4 hrs - 6 hours More than 6 hours (Don't know)	(107) 1 2 3 4 5 6 7	

23

		Col./ Code	Skip to

5.

a) SHOW CARD A

Which parts of the Visitor Centre shown on
this card did you go to on this visit ?
CODE IN a) OF GRID BELOW,   OR ————→ None visited

	(108)	
	1	Q.6

FOR EACH VISITED, ASK b) AND SHOW CARD B

b) How did you like the ... (PART
VISITED) ? Which of the phrases
on this card best describes how
you feel about it ?

	Cafe	Shop	Robin Hood Exhibition	Studio
a) Visited :	A	B	C	D
	(109)	(110)	(111)	(112)
b) Liked a lot	1	1	1	1
Liked a little	2	2	2	2
Neither liked nor disliked it	3	3	3	3
Disliked a little	4	4	4	4
Disliked a lot	5	5	5	5
Not applicable (did not visit)	N	N	N	N

6.a) Did you or anyone in your party spend
any money in the Visitor Centre today?

	(113)	
Yes	1	
No	2	Q.7

IF 'YES' (CODE 1 AT a), ASK b) AND c)

b) In which parts of the Visitor Centre
did you or your party spend money ?

ONE CODE ONLY

	(114)
Shop only	1
Cafe only	2
Both shop and cafe	3

c) How much money have you and your party
spent altogether in the Visitor Centre
today on this visit ?

WRITE IN TO NEAREST £ [ ]   (115-16)
(DO NOT WRITE IN THE PENCE,
ROUND UP IF 50p OR OVER)

	(117)
OR CODE →Less than 50p	1

7. Have you been to the Visitor Centre before on
a previous visit, or was this the first time?

	(118)
Been before	1
First time	2

8. Is this your first visit to Sherwood Forest
or nave you been here before?

	(119)	
First visit	1	
Visited before	2	Q.14

		Col./Code	Skip to
IF ON <u>FIRST, EVER VISIT</u> ASK Q.9 - 13 BELOW			

9.a) How did you first come to hear about Sherwood Forest Country Park as a place to visit?

<u>DO NOT PROMPT.</u> <u>PROBE AS NECESSARY</u>

ONE CODE ONLY

	Col./Code	Skip to
	(120)	
'Just always knew'	1	
Word of mouth - from friends/relatives	2	
Tourist information (eg told by hotel/TIC)	3	Q.10
Guidebook	4	
Advertisement/poster	5	
Newspaper article	6	
Radio/TV programme	7	
Saw a sign outside/drove past	8	Q.10
	0	

Other (WRITE IN) _____

(121)

IF CODES 5 OR 6 AT a), ASK b) AND c)

b) Where did you see the advert/poster/newspaper article?

<u>PROBE FULLY</u>

c) Was this a factor that made you decide to visit Sherwood today?

	Col./Code
	(122)
Yes	1
No	2

10. How long ago did you first hear of Sherwood Forest as a place to visit?

	Col./Code
	(123)
Within the last month	1
More than one month - 6 months ago	2
More than six months - 1 year ago	3
More than one year - 2 years ago	4
More than 2 years ago	5

		Col./ Code	Skip to

FIRST TIME VISITORS ONLY

11.a) And what was it that prompted you to
visit Sherwood now on this trip?

PROBE FULLY   Any other reasons?

What was it that made you want to come here?

Why have you come here now as opposed to any other time?

RECORD VERBATIM

b) Which of these would you say was the main
reason for your choosing to come here to Sherwood
Forest? PROBE FULLY AND RECORD VERBATIM.

FIRST TIME VISITORS ONLY

12.a) I'd like you to think back now to what you expected Sherwood Forest Country Park to be like before your visit today. Has it turned out to be more or less as you expected it to be, or are there some ways in which it is different?

	(124)	
As expected	1	Q.13
Different	2	

IF 'DIFFERENT' (CODE 2 AT a), ASK b) - d)

b) In what ways is it different from what you expected?

   PROBE FULLY   Are there any other things that are different?

   RECORD VERBATIM

c) What do you think gave you this picture of what it would be like before you came here?

   PROBE FULLY

   MORE THAN ONE ANSWER MAY BE CODED

	(125)
Knowledge of other sites/parks/forests visited	1
Robin Hood legend/Robin Hood books or films	2
Hearsay from other people/friends/relatives	3
Printed descriptions (posters/magazines/newspapers etc)	4
Other (SPECIFY) _____	
_____	9
_____	

d) So on balance would you say that it is better or worse than you expected it to be?

	(126)
Better	1
Worse	2

		Col./ Code	Skip to

FIRST TIME VISITORS ONLY   - 6 -

13.   Do you think you will come here   (127)
      again on a future visit?   Yes   1   Q.20
                                                    No   2

      IF NO (CODE 2 AT a), ASK b)

      b) Why do you say that?
          PROBE FULLY AND RECORD VERBATIM

                    NOW GO TO Q.20 (page 10)

		Col./Code	Skip to

IF VISITED SHERWOOD BEFORE ASK Q.14-19 BELOW

14. Not counting this visit, how many times have you been here before?

	Col./Code
	(128)
Once before	1
Twice	2
3 times	3
4 times	4
5-9 times	5
10 times or more	6

15. And when was your <u>first</u> visit here?

	Col./Code
	(129)
Within the last month	1
More than one month - 6 months ago	2
More than six months - 1 year ago	3
More than one year - 2 years ago	4
More than two years - 5 years ago	5
Five or more years ago	6

16. Thinking back, how did you <u>first</u> hear about Sherwood as a place to visit?

<u>DO NOT PROMPT.</u>   PROBE AS NECESSARY

ONE CODE ONLY

	Col./Code
	(130)
'Just always knew'	1
Word of mouth - from friends/relatives	2
Tourist information (eg told by hotel/TIC)	3
Guidebook	4
Advertisement/poster	5
Newspaper article	6
Radio/TV programme	7
Saw a sign outside/drove past	8
	0

Other (WRITE IN) _____

	(131)

	REPEAT VISITORS ONLY	Col./ Code	Skip to

17.a) What was it that prompted you to visit
Sherwood now on this trip?

PROBE FULLY   Any other reasons?

Why have you come here today?

RECORD VERBATIM

b) Which of these would you say was the
main reason for your choosing to come
here to Sherwood today?

PROBE FULLY AND RECORD VERBATIM

		Col./ Code	Skip to
	REPEAT VISITORS ONLY		
18.	Since you've been here more than once, what is it about the Park that makes you choose to <u>come back</u> here? <u>PROBE FULLY</u> Why have you come back <u>here</u> as opposed to somewhere else? <u>RECORD VERBATIM</u>		
19.	Would you say that you are ever influenced by any publicity material about the park - such as posters or leaflets or articles etc - in making you decide to revisit it?		
	Yes	(132) 1	
	No	2	

	Col./ Code	Skip to

ASK ALL

20. Roughly how often, on average, do you take day or half day trips into the country or to places or interest round about?

(133)

	Col./ Code	Skip to
More frequently than once a week	1	
Once a week	2	
2/3 times a month	3	
Once a month	4	
Several times a year but less frequently than once a month	5	
Once a year	6	
Less frequently than once a year	7	

	Col./Code	Skip to

ASK ALL

21.a) During the past 6 months or so, have you read or heard about Sherwood Forest Country Park in any of these ways ... READ OUT EACH ITEM

CODE YES OR NO FOR EACH

	YES	NO
... Poster/leaflet - in a library	1	A
- in a hotel	2	B
- in a Tourist Information Centre	3	C
Advertisement in the newspaper	4	D
Mentioned - on local radio	5	E
- on television	6	F
NONE OF ABOVE	7	

(134) — NONE OF ABOVE → Q.22

IF ANY OF CODES 1-3 MARKED (YES) AT a) ASK b)-d)

b) Was it a poster or a leaflet that you saw in the ... (library/hotel/Tourist Information Centre).

MORE THAN ONE MAY BE CODED

(135)
Poster	1
Leaflet	2
Other	3
Can't remember	9

IF ANY OF CODES 1-6 MARKED (YES) AT a)

c) What was/were the poster(s) (/advertisement(s)/feature(s)) like? Can you describe them to me? PROBE FULLY

MORE THAN ONE MAY BE CODED

(136)
Advertising - a specific exhibition	1
- a special event (eg sports event/treasure hunt)	2
- guided walks/tours	3
- the Craft Centre/Visitor Centre	4
Any mention of Robin Hood	5

Other (WRITE IN) _____

_____

_____ Can't remember 9

d) Did it/they appeal to you and make you want to visit the Park?

(137)
Yes	1
No	2
(Not applicable because would visit the Park anyway)	3	Q.22

e) Would you say that it/they influenced you in your decision to visit Sherwood today on this trip?

(138)
Yes	1
No	2
(Don't know)	9

			Col./ Code	Skip to

22.a) I am going to read a few statements that people have made about Sherwood Forest. Please say whether you agree or disagree with each of them by choosing one of the phrases from this card. SHOW CARD C. ROTATE ORDER OF READING OUT STATEMENTS AND RECORD STARTING STATEMENT BY CODING LETTER IN LEFT HAND COLUMN.

START		Agree		Neither agree nor disagree	Disagree		Col./ Code
		Strongly	Slightly		Slightly	Strongly	
	Sherwood Forest is ...						
A	... a place where you can enjoy <u>true</u> <u>countryside</u>	1	2	3	4	5	(139)
B	... a good place to visit with friends <u>or</u> <u>relatives</u>	1	2	3	4	5	(140)
C	... a place to learn about the forest and <u>nature</u>	1	2	3	4	5	(141)
D	... less a place for adults, more a place for children	1	2	3	4	5	(142)
E	... a place to get away from urban built-up areas	1	2	3	4	5	(143)
F	... a place to get away from large numbers of people	1	2	3	4	5	(144)
G	... a place to get away from commercialism	1	2	3	4	5	(145)

		Col./ Code	Skip to

Now I'd like to ask a few questions about what made you decide to come here today.

23. First of all, when did you make the decision to come here to Sherwood on this visit: was it on the spur of the moment today or was it longer ago than that?

(146)

Today - after setting out	1
Today - before setting out	2
Yesterday	3
2-3 days ago	4
4 days - a week ago	5
8 days - 2 weeks ago	6
15 days - a month ago	7

PROBE AND PROMPT IF NECESSARY.

ONE CODE ONLY

Longer ago (SPECIFY) _____ 8

24. Who would you say made the decision to come here today? PROBE IF NECESSARY

(147)

Respondent	1
Spouse	2
Child(ren) - under 15 yrs	3
Child(ren) - 16+ yrs	4

Other member of party (SPECIFY) _____ 5

Other (SPECIFY) _____ 6

Finally, I'd like to ask a few questions about yourself and the people with you on this visit.

25.a) How many people, including yourself, are there in your party?　　WRITE IN: [ ][ ]　(148-49)
(USE LEADING ZERO)

b) And how many including yourself are in each age group. WRITE IN NUMBERS IN COLUMN b). CHECK BREAKDOWN b) EQUALS TOTAL NUMBER WRITTEN IN AT a). SHOW CARD D IF NECESSARY

c) And which is your own age group? RECORD IN COLUMN c)

	b)	c)
- 2 years	(150)	Respondent's Age
3-5	(151)	
6-10	(152)	
11-15	(153)	(158)
16-24	(154)	1
25-44	(155)	2
45-59	(156)	3
60+	(157)	4

	Col./ Code	Skip to
Q 26 REFERS TO THE HOH		
ESTABLISH WHETHER RESPONDENT IS HOH ────────→ Respondent is HOH	(159) 1	
It has been found that people in different types of jobs have different interests in countryside recreation. To help us plan for this, can I ask ... Not HOH	2	
26. a) ... are you (is the head of the household) in paid employment at present ?	(160)	
Yes : Working full-time (30+ hours)	1	
ASK ABOUT HOH Working part-time (10-29 hours)	2	
Working part-time (under 10 hours)	3	
No : Seeking work	4	
wholly retired	5	
full-time student	6	} Q.27
Non-working housewife, no paid work	7	
Other (SPECIFY) _____	8	

b) IF IN PAID EMPLOYMENT ASK ABOUT PRESENT JOB.
IF SEEKING WORK ASK ABOUT LAST JOB.
IF RETIRED ASK ABOUT MAIN JOB.

Name of job : _____

Description of activity : _____

_____

_____

Qualifications for job : _____

_____

Management/supervision : _____

_____

Industry : _____

No. of people employed at place of work : _____

| Employee/self-employed :   Employee | A |
| Self employed | B |

27. And finally do you own or have the use of a car ?	(161)	
Yes	1	
No	2	

INTERVIEWER TO CODE :	(162)
Sex of respondent : Male	1
Female	2

THANK YOU VERY MUCH FOR YOUR HELP	Time interview ended (24 hr clock) hour mins	(163-66)
Interviewer's name :	Length of interview: minutes	(167-68) (169)
_____	Day of week : Friday	1
Interviewer's No :	Saturday	2
▯▯▯▯	Sunday	3
	Fieldwork Phase: 3	(170)